MW01102104

MASTER THIS!

Filmmaking

Todd Downing

PowerKiDS
press.

New York

Published in 2011 by The Rosen Publishing Group Inc.
29 East 21st Street, New York, NY 10010

First Edition

Commissioning Editor: Jennifer Sanderson
Senior Editor: Claire Shanahan
Produced by Tall Tree Ltd.
Editor, Tall Tree: Jon Richards
Designer: Ed Simkins
Artwork: The Apple Agency

Downey, Todd.
   Filmmaking / by Todd Downey. -- 1st ed.
      p. cm. -- (Master this!)
   Includes index.
   ISBN 978-1-61532-597-9 (library binding)
   ISBN 978-1-61532-602-0 (paperback)
   ISBN 978-1-61532-603-7 (6-pack)
   1. Motion pictures--Production and direction--Juvenile
   literature. I. Title.
   PN1995.9.P7D695 2011
   791.4302'3--dc22
                                                     2009045759

Manufactured in China
CPSIA Compliance Information: Batch #WAS0102PK: For Further Information
contact Rosen Publishing, New York, New York at 1-800-237-9932

Photographs
All photographs taken by Michael Wicks, except:
t-top, b-bottom, l-left, r-right, c-center
Front cover istockphoto.com/Alexei Tacu
5 Bettmann/Corbis, 7b Colin Swan, 8t Biserka Livaja/
Corbis, 13t Dreamstime.com/Tea, 13b Dreamstime.com/
Michael Flippo, 14br Dreamstime.com/Teslenko Petro,
16 Sarah Ruocco, 17cl Dreamstime.com/Szczepko,
17bl Dreamstime.com/Barsik, 17tr and br Dreamstime.
com/Darren Baker, 19cl Dreamstime.com/Olga
Demchishina, 19bl Dreamstime.com/Luminis, 19br
Dreamstime.com/Soundsnaps, 21bl Dreamstime.com/
Elpis Ioannidis, 21br Dreamstime.com/Andres Rodriguez,
23b Lucy Nicholson/Reuters/Corbis, 24cb Dreamstime.
com, 24br Dreamstime.com/Jeanne Hatch, 25bl Stephane
Cardinale/People Avenue/Corbis, 26b Pierre Verdy/AFP/
Getty Images, 29 Dreasmtime.com/Onestepbeyond

Disclaimer
In preparation of this book, all due care has been
exercised with regard to the advice, activities, and
techniques depicted. The publishers regret that they
can accept no liability for any loss or injury sustained.
When learning a new skill, it is important to get expert
instruction and to follow a manufacturer's guidelines.

Acknowledgements
The publishers would like to thank Chad Brown, Lucy
Pisapia, and Tom Jordan for their help with this book.

Contents

Making Movies

Today, films can be made using a wide range of equipment. Technology has progressed so much since the early days of filmmaking that anyone can make and **distribute** a movie.

Movies for All

The earliest movies were made using expensive and heavy equipment. Highly trained people were needed to operate the camera and poisonous chemicals were used to **develop** the film. Now anyone with a camera phone and a home computer can be a director and show their movies to the world. Even though the tools of filmmaking have changed, the basic principles are the same.

Today, movie cameras are so small that they can be built into cell phones. This technology means that you can make basic movies almost anywhere you go.

Modern big-**budget** movies, such as this James Bond film, still need expensive equipment to film them and a large crowd of people to work on them. These include the actors who perform in front of the camera and the **crew** that works behind the scenes.

Types of Movies

There are many different types of movie. Narrative films tell a story and are what you normally see at the movie theater. Documentary films, such as *Fahrenheit 9/11* or *March of the Penguins*, attempt to capture reality by filming "real" events and people. Experimental filmmakers avoid traditional stories and try to create new ways of looking at the world. Music videos, which grew largely out of experimental film, put images to music and songs. In animated movies, characters and locations can be created with computers, as in Pixar's *Wall-E*, or they can be made out of clay, as they are in Aardman Animations' Wallace and Gromit movies.

Film Development

Filmmaking is divided into five stages: development, preproduction, production, postproduction, and distribution. In development, you write the **screenplay** and find money to fund the project.

Top Tip

When writing a screenplay, remember that this is not the same as writing a play or a novel. For example, you can show that a character is angry in a close-up of the actor's eyes, rather than having them say, "I'm angry!"

The Screenplay

Also known as the script, the screenplay tells the movie's story on paper. Some types of film, such as documentaries, do not have a screenplay, but that does not mean they should not have an outline. Like narrative films, it is necessary to know at least whom you want to film and where you want to film them. The outline should detail how you want the shots to appear in your movie.

A properly formatted screenplay will have one page of action for every minute of the film. It shows who the characters are, what they say, what they do, and where they do it.

scene information

character

dialogue

action

```
EXT. CORSICA MOUNTAINSIDE - NIGHT

A small car is driving along the treacherous windy roads
of the French island.
                                                    CUT TO:


INT. AUTOMOBILE - NIGHT

JULES - a middle aged woman - and RICHARD - her husband -
are arguing. Their sons DAVID and BEN, 8-year-old twins,
are in the back. French pop music plays on the radio.

                        JULES
                     (to Richard)
            Stop it! Why are you always criticizing
            me? This is the way we're supposed to go!

                        RICHARD
            Fine, fine. Whatever you want to do.
            Always what you want to do. Your French
            is perfect so I'm sure you understood
            the directions perfectly.

                        JULES
            Richard, enough with the sarcasm!
            Try and be helpful for once instead
            of making things worse.

As their parents argue, David and Ben remain silent in
the back seat. David stares out of the window and into
the night seemingly unaware of the commotion in the front.
Suddenly, his eyes widen and a burst of colored light
flashes across his face. We hear a loud SCREECH OF TYRES
and SCREAMS.
                                                    CUT TO:


EXT. CORSICA ROADSIDE - NIGHT

The car has swirled around the road, evidenced by skid
marks. A shadowy figure lies on the ground in front of
the car, slowly moving. It is not discernible whether
it's human or not.
                                                    CUT TO:


INT. AUTOMOBILE - NIGHT

Everyone in the car is safe, but stunned. The radio
continues to play French pop music. Ben is crying.
```

It is helpful to hear a screenplay read aloud by actors a few times before you shoot the film. This is called a reading. Dialogue, or what the actors say, can sound very different when it is spoken from how it appears on the page.

Star File

WOODY ALLEN
Comic Genius

Woody Allen has made an average of one feature a year since the mid-1960s, many set in Manhattan, New York City. He is known for funny dialogue that is so individual, critics invented the term "Allenesque" to refer to other filmmakers who copy him. Over his 40-year career, Allen has received 21 Oscar nominations, but he has so little respect for the way the film industry operates that he has shown up to the ceremonies only twice.

Funding

Another part of development is finding money to fund your movie. It is the responsibility of the movie's producer to find money and decide on the best way to spend it. Funding can come from friends and family, your own savings or, on a more professional level, from arts funding groups or movie studios. When writing your screenplay, keep in mind how much money you have to spend. If you have very little, keep the story simple, using only a few locations and characters.

Preproduction

Preproduction is where you carefully map out your shoot, find all the necessary people you need to complete your film, and make a schedule and a budget.

Scenes and Schedules

The first step in preproduction is to break down your screenplay into scenes. A scene is the action that takes place in one location for a continuous time. Scenes are numbered in the order they appear in a screenplay. After ordering your scenes, you can make a shot list. This is a list of scenes, with their location, action, and dialogue. You then organize your shot list into a shooting schedule, listing where and when you plan to shoot each scene.

A shooting schedule shows what scenes are being shot on which day, and the actors and props needed. To save money, shoot all the scenes in one location at the same time.

Day/Date	Scene	INT/TEXT, Day/Night	Shot description	Location	Characters	Art department, Equipment, Special requirements
SHOOT DAY 1		TUES 31 MARCH 2009				
08:00–08:30		Cast & Crew arrive, breakfast		23 Tulip Road, Essex		
09:00–10:15	6	EXT, Night	Jules, Richard, John and Ben pack up the car	Jules' house in Essex	Jules, Richard, John, Ben	Car, luggage
10:15–13:00	7	INT, Night	Family drives to airport	White Hart Lane	Jules, Richard, John, Ben	Car
13:00–14:00		lunch				
14:00–16:30	2	EXT, Day	Jules leaves work in London	Chelmsford	Jules	Dolly
16:30–18:30	1	INT, Day	Jules at her desk	Law offices, Chelmsford	Jules	Dolly
18:30	wrap					

Drawing a Storyboard

Another helpful tool in preproduction is the storyboard. A storyboard is an illustration of the movie, drawn by a storyboard artist. It can be very useful in making sure everyone understands what the film should look like. Do not worry if you do not have a storyboard artist to draw your storyboard. Even the simplest drawings with stick figures are helpful in figuring out how a film is to be shot.

Top Tip

Make sure you figure out an estimate of the costs for each stage of your movie before you start filming. This is called the budget. Using spreadsheet computer software will help you to keep your costs under control.

Storyboards

The director tells the storyboard artist how she wants the movie to be shot, giving him as much detail as possible.

The artist then completes the storyboard, adding details such as the scene number and summary of action.

Direction: Wide shot—all characters are in view.
Text: No text, music playing.

Direction: Pan across characters left to right.
Text: "Where were you last night?"

The finished storyboard will look a little like a cartoon strip, with notes added so that each person involved in the movie knows what he or she is doing.

Casting and Crew

Art films or low-budget documentaries are sometimes put together by just one person. However, filmmaking is usually a team effort, involving a cast (the actors) and the crew.

Choosing Actors

Casting is the process of choosing actors to appear in a movie. On films with large budgets, this process is organized by a casting director. He or she brings the director photographs of actors, lists of their previous work, and **showreels** of other performances. The director picks their favorites and holds an **audition**. Auditions are often videotaped, so the director has a record when discussing whom to cast.

Casting

The director and casting director look at photographs of different actors and choose the ones they want to see at an audition.

At an audition, the actors read from the screenplay in front of the director so that he or she can choose whom to cast.

Rehearsing

A rehearsal is when the cast practices how to act out a scene under the guidance of the director. Even though this can be done on **set** just before shooting a scene, you should make every effort to schedule some rehearsal time in the weeks before the shoot. Actors need time to "find," or figure out how to perform, their characters, and you as director will need time to guide them there.

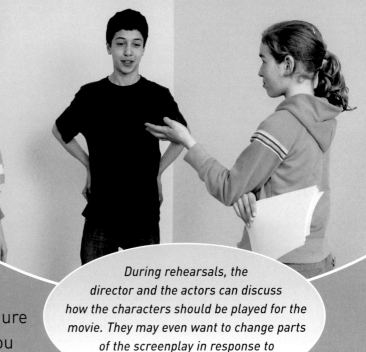

During rehearsals, the director and the actors can discuss how the characters should be played for the movie. They may even want to change parts of the screenplay in response to some comments.

The Crew

The size of a crew is largely determined by budget and can range anywhere from one person to hundreds of people. Below is a list of some of the key crew roles. However, you do not need to employ all these people to make your movie. Some of these roles can be performed by one person or may not be needed at all on smaller productions.

THE DIRECTOR (also known as "the filmmaker") directs the film, guiding the actors and the rest of the crew.

THE PRODUCER finds funding, oversees the hiring of the crew, and finds distribution.

THE DIRECTOR OF PHOTOGRAPHY (also known as a "cinematographer" or DoP) oversees the camera and lighting department and operates the camera (larger productions will have a separate "camera operator").

THE ASSISTANT DIRECTOR (or AD) manages the set and makes sure the shoot is running to schedule.

THE PRODUCTION DESIGNER ensures the sets and other elements all work together visually.

THE COSTUME DESIGNER is responsible for the costumes and clothing the actors wear.

HAIR AND MAKEUP ARTISTS create and maintain the hairstyles and makeup of the actors.

THE SOUND RECORDIST is responsible for recording the sound on set. They communicate with the boom operator, who holds and positions the microphone.

THE GAFFER is the head of the electrical department and places the lights.

THE GRIP moves and secures the equipment and props on a set. There are also speciality grips such as "dolly grips," who operate equipment such as dollies (wheeled vehicles that cameras can be mounted on to make a shot look like it is floating).

A PRODUCTION ASSISTANT is an entry-level role that involves many basic jobs.

The Camera

Once you have made a budget, shot list, and shooting schedule, and picked your cast and crew, you are ready to choose equipment. The choices are vast and will be decided by the type of movie you want to shoot and your budget.

Types of Camera

Cameras can be divided into three groups: tape, film, and tapeless. Today, the most common cameras use tape to record moving images. It is the standard for low-budget films, television, and documentaries. These cameras record digital video (DV) or high-definition video (HDV) onto a miniDV tape. HDV cameras give better picture quality than DV, but they are usually more expensive.

foldout screen

mount for a light

battery

hand strap

record button

HDV cameras

microphone clip

camera lens

eyepiece

tape door

focusing ring

Tapeless Video

A recent development in filmmaking is tapeless video recording. Tapeless cameras record video straight onto a computer hard disk or flash memory card. This is the technology your cell phone camera uses to record videos, but the same type of technology can also be used in professional cameras for **feature films**.

memory card

Film Cameras

Before the invention of video, recording onto film stock was the only way to film moving images. Film stock is made of a thin strip of flexible plastic called **celluloid**. A strip of film is split into thousands of individual rectangles, called frames. When the frames are run quickly through a **projector**, they give the impression that the picture is moving.

Film stock and developing are expensive, but digital video is cheaper and easy to use. For these reasons, film is used less and less. But many filmmakers prefer to use film, because it can capture a wide range of detail.

Lenses and Support

In addition to the camera, there are several other important pieces of equipment needed to shoot your movie, including camera support and lenses.

Camera Support

Cameras can be held in the hands, but for a smoother shot with less **camera shake**, they need some form of support, such as a tripod or a dolly. A tripod is a camera support with three legs. The camera fixes, or mounts, onto a tripod head, which sits on the legs. Tripods will give you a very solid, still image and should allow you to perform smooth pans (turning from side to side) and tilts (moving up and down).

A tripod gets its name from the fact that it has three ("tri-") legs. These give a solid base on which to fix the camera.

Dollies

A dolly is a wheeled piece of equipment that runs on tracks to allow for smooth camera movements. Dollies make the camera feel like it is floating along and are used for most big movie productions.

14

Here, the camera is pressed to the shoulder while looking through the eyepiece.

Here, the camera is pressed to the shoulder while looking at the foldout screen.

Here, for a steadier image, the camera is cradled firmly in the hands.

Lenses

The lens is the camera's eye. It allows light into the camera and focuses the image, making it appear sharp. Some cameras have interchangeable lenses, but the cheapest models have a set lens that cannot be changed. **Focal length** determines the angle of view for a lens and how far away objects are when they are in focus. Changing the focal length while shooting is called zooming.

Focal Lengths

A wide-angle lens produces an image wider than the human eye would see. A medium focal length lens mimics what you would see naturally. A telephoto lens makes far-away objects appear closer.

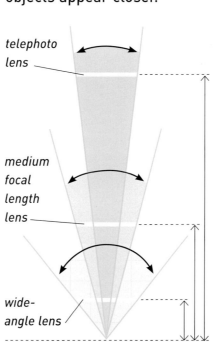

telephoto lens

medium focal length lens

wide-angle lens

camera

This image was taken using a wide-angle lens.

A medium focal length lens captured this image.

This image was taken using a telephoto lens.

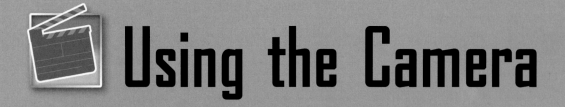

Using the Camera

Production is the stage of filmmaking where you use the camera. Although all cameras operate differently, some of their basic functions are the same.

Setting Up the Camera

The first step is to load the batteries into your camera. Next, load a tape into the camera, making sure that you close the tape door lightly since they can be quite fragile. If you are using a tripod, screw the plate from the tripod into the bottom of the camera. Place the camera onto the tripod and lock the plate into the head.

Top Tip

Keep a spare set of charged camera batteries on hand, in case the first set runs flat. Do not recharge your batteries until they are totally flat, because constant recharging wears them down.

When the camera is set up, the viewfinder will show the image it is recording as well as information such as battery life and time.

battery charge level

recording mode

■ | | |185 min   ● REC   02:51:34:16

central crosshatch

50%

3900K   F2.8   CH1
                                                 CH2

white balance indicator   f-stop indicator   audio meters

Adjusting the Camera

Once the camera is on the tripod, adjust the white balance to suit the lighting. Select Tungsten or the light bulb symbol if your light source is tungsten-balanced, or Daylight or the Sun symbol if your main source of light is the Sun. If the lighting is mixed, hold a white card in front of the camera and zoom in so that white fills the frame, then press the White Balance button. This will adjust the white balance to the **color temperature** (see page 18) of the scene. Next, set the exposure by adjusting the aperture. The aperture controls how much light is let into the camera and is measured in "f-stops." Finally, adjust the focus so that the image is sharp.

(see page 18)

Focusing

An out-of-focus image will appear blurred.

Turn the focusing ring just behind the lens to focus. Zoom in to focus, then pull out to frame the image.

When in focus, the image will appear sharp.

F-stops

A small f-stop setting, such as f/4, is used for dark, indoor shots where there is very little light.

A high f-stop setting, such as f/22, is used for bright, outdoor shots where there is a lot of light.

Lights and Microphones

Lighting and sound can be just as important, if not more so, than the type of camera you use. Time spent thinking about these will result in a much better movie.

Changing Lights

We see most light as white, but different types of light actually have different colors or color temperatures. Daylight is bluish in color, while the lights in our homes, or tungsten-balanced lights, are more yellow. You can change the color temperature by using gels. These are sheets of colored plastic that are clipped over the front of the lights.

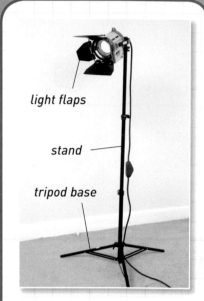

light flaps

stand

tripod base

Small lights are fitted to a stand. Larger lights will need strong **rigging** to lift them high above the cast and crew.

This blue gel changes tungsten-balanced lights into daylight-balanced lights. An orange gel will do the opposite.

*This **diffusion** will soften the light. You can also soften light by bouncing it off a wall or a white board.*

Microphones and Sound Recording

Microphones, or "mics" for short, capture the sound of the scene you are shooting. They are categorized by the directions in which they pick up sound and include omnidirectional mics and supercardioid mics (see below). The microphones collect the sound and convert it into electrical signals, which are then recorded by the sound recordist or directly onto the video tape.

Types of Microphone

OMNI

Omnidirectional mics record sound from all around them. They will pick up all sounds on your set, from behind, as well as in front of, the camera.

An omnidirectional mic picks up sound from all directions.

SHOTGUN

Supercardioid, or shotgun, mics record sound mainly from the direction in which they are pointed.

Shotgun mic records sound mostly from in front.

WIRELESS

Wireless mics are small microphones that are clipped to an actor's shirt. The sound is sent wirelessly via radio waves back to the sound recordist.

BOOM

A boom is a long pole to which a microphone can be fitted at one end. This allows the mic to be held close to the actors, but without being in the picture.

The Shoot

There is no single way to make your film. How you choose to shoot it will make your movie unique. However, there are some basics rules you should follow to ensure that you get the footage you need.

Blocking and Coverage

When you are on set, the first thing to think about is how the action will occur in the scene. Will the actors remain still? Or will they move and, if so, will the camera follow them? Run through the scene and figure out what works best. This is called "blocking" or "blocking out the scene." Coverage refers to the amount of footage you shoot and the different angles you shoot from. Cover a scene from different angles and framings to give yourself options when you edit.

Top Tip

Do not use the autofocus while shooting your scene. If the actors or camera are moving and the autofocus is set, the camera will continually readjust the focus and ruin your shot.

Coverage

To get a choice of shots, first shoot a scene in a wide shot, where the actors are visible from head to toe.

Next, shoot the scene again, this time in a medium shot, showing the actors from the knees up.

Finally, shoot the scene again, this time in close up, where the actors' heads take up most of the screen.

180 Degree Rule

When you are shooting coverage, use the 180 degree rule. For instance, when two characters are positioned on the left and right of the frame, the left-hand character should stay on the left, and the right-hand character on the right. Imagine a line running between the characters. The camera should not cross this line, which limits the angles you can shoot from to 180 degrees.

The Rule of Thirds

The rule of thirds states that a picture looks best when the main elements sit one-third of the way in from the frame's edges. For example, in a close-up of a face, the eyes should fall one-third of the way from the top of the image.

180 Degree Rule

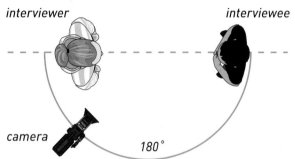

interviewer *interviewee*

camera *180°*

When filming two characters, you should avoid crossing a line on the floor between the two actors. Breaking the 180 degree rule is called "crossing the line."

Rule of Thirds

Here, the top of the cliff face on which the ruined temple is sitting lies about one-third of the way down from the top.

Similarly, in this picture, the girls' eyes are positioned one-third from the top. The other third lines are shown in red.

Shooting the Scene

There is a standard procedure for shooting a scene. The assistant director (AD) and director will call out a series of directions to make sure that everyone is ready for the action to be filmed.

Getting Ready

First, the AD calls out "final checks" so that the crew can check the equipment, the actors can position themselves, and the hair, makeup, and wardrobe departments can make sure the actors look right. The AD asks for everyone to be quiet and then tells each of the crew to start their equipment. Someone then claps the slate (see page 23) in front of the camera, the AD calls "action" and the scene begins.

This group of people involved in shooting a scene includes two actors (1), a sound recordist holding a microphone on a boom (2), an assistant director (3), the director of photography (4), and the director (5).

The Slate

Clapping the slate together gives the editor a visual and audio clue to line up pictures and sound.

ROLL	SCENE	TAKE
3	2	5

DIRECTOR Lauren Hardy

CAMERA OPERATOR Siobhan Adair

DATE 16/04/09   (DAY)   NIGHT

A slate, or clapperboard, is used to synchronize the picture and the sound for a film if they are recorded separately. The slate also has information written on it, including which "take" it is. Takes are numbered versions of the same shot. Numbering helps the editor to organize footage (see page 24).

Star File

PETER JACKSON
Hobbits and Rings

Shooting almost exclusively in New Zealand, Peter Jackson is best known for directing the *Lord of the Rings* trilogy. Jackson has had passionate fans following his work since the late 1980s, when he began making low-budget comic-horror films with his friends. It was his originality and ingenuity that caught the eyes of the big studios and catapulted him into becoming one of the highest-paid directors in the industry.

Taking Your Time

Never rush the actors into performing a scene right after calling "action." Let them take their time and begin acting when they feel it is right for them. After the scene ends, the director calls "cut." Only then does the camera stop recording and the actors come out of character. However, do not rush calling "cut" right after a scene is over. You are not yet sure how you want to edit your film and you may need extra footage (see pages 24–25).

Film Editing

Postproduction, or "post," occurs after the shoot. The first step in postproduction is film editing. This is the process where the film editor puts shots together to make sequences, and the sequences together to make a movie.

Capturing Your Footage

In order to edit, you first need to capture the footage into the editing software on your computer. Connect your camera to the computer with a firewire cable. Open the capture tool in your editing software and use it to cue, or move, the tape to the beginning of the first take. Mark an **in point** and then cue the tape to the end of the first take and mark an out point. Now click on the Capture button. This segment of footage between the "in" and "out" is called a clip. Repeat this for each take until all your clips are captured.

*Scenes and sequences are edited together using film-editing software. At the bottom of the screen is the **timeline**, which shows all of the different clips as they are put together into sequences.*

These two screens, or monitors, show the timeline and individual clips.

bins and folders

clips

timeline

Editing into the Timeline

The timeline shows the order and length of the clips in your edit. Mark an in and an out point on the clip you like. Now edit this clip—we will call this "Clip A"—into the timeline by hitting the Insert Edit button. Find the clip you want to appear next in the timeline, "Clip B," and mark your "in" and "out." In the timeline, also mark an "in" where you want the clip to begin and click on Insert Edit again. You now have two clips in a row, and are starting to build a sequence.

Star File

SOFIA COPPOLA
Actor to Director

Daughter of directing legend, Francis Ford Coppola, Sofia started her film career in front of the camera, appearing in *The Outsiders* and *The Godfather: Part 3*. She made an impact as a director with the 1999 movie *The Virgin Suicides*, and became only the third female director to be Oscar nominated with her 2003 feature *Lost in Translation*.

Insert and Overwrite Edits

Here, two clips, A and B, form a sequence.

The editor wants to insert clip C between them, and so performs an insert edit. Clip B is pushed later to make room for clip C.

The clip order is now A, C, B.

Here, the editor starts with the sequence of clip A followed by clip B.

She wants to perform an overwrite edit to replace scene B with scene C.

The new scene order is clip A followed by clip C.

Editing Sound

Sound, or audio, is often neglected, even though it makes up half the filmgoing experience. Good sound editing can enhance the mood you are trying to create in your movie.

Editing the Sound

Sound editing is very similar to picture editing in that you load a sound clip, select an "in" and an "out," and then edit it into the timeline. The big difference is the number of tracks you will have—there will be many more audio tracks than video tracks. Feature films can have more than 100 audio tracks.

Types of Sound

There are many different types of sound used in filmmaking:

DIALOGUE is what the actors say and is recorded on set.

VOICE-OVER acts as narration or to indicate a character's thoughts.

SOUND EFFECTS are added to emphasize an event in a scene, such as glass breaking or a gun firing.

FOLEYS are sounds produced manually to match an event in a movie, such as the sound of galloping horses created by banging together coconut shells.

BACKGROUND AMBIENCES are sounds in the film that do not represent anything in particular on screen but are used to make the film feel more natural or to create a mood, such as rain or wind.

Many of a film's audio tracks are recorded after the images have been recorded. Here, the French actors Philippe Peythieu and Véronique Augereau record a voice-over in a studio.

Sound Mix

The sound mix—or simply, "mix"—is the process of adjusting the audio tracks against each other to produce the final sound for your film. The mix allows you to alter the loudness of each of the audio tracks. You should avoid having the mix too loud because this could distort the audio. Another purpose of the mix is to smooth out transitions between audio clips. An easy way to do this is to add "fades" on the beginning and end of each audio clip. Audio fades gradually raise the volume of a clip from silence or lower it to silence. Without these, you may hear a "click" or a "pop" when a new audio clip begins.

Here, a foley artist is recording a foley by scrunching audio tape to mimic the sound of walking through dry leaves.

Top Tip

Be careful not to use voice-over to point out what is obviously happening in a scene. If the audience can see what is going on, it does not need to be told it, too.

Audio Levels

Your editing software should have an audio meter so you can judge the loudness of your sound. The meter is colored from green to red, and you want the levels to stay roughly where the green changes to yellow.

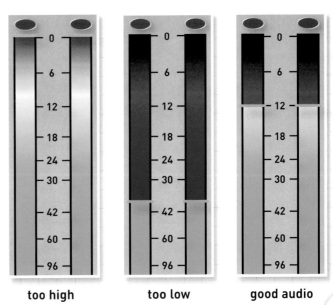

too high   too low   good audio

Taking It Further

Having made your movie, you are now ready to show it. You will also want to start thinking about making your next film and learning more about the whole filmmaking experience.

The Internet is a great place to show your films. You can upload movies to film-sharing web sites, after getting permission from the actors and your parents.

Getting It Seen

Distribution is the final step in filmmaking and is the process of making your movie available to the public. This can be at movie theaters, on television, video stores, or the Internet. A company that distributes movies is called a distributor, and it is responsible for getting the film into theaters as well as the advertising, posters, and DVD packaging. Film festivals offer independent filmmakers not only an audience, but also the chance to sell their movies to distributors who look for films at festivals.

Top Tip

When you apply to a festival, you will usually have to fill out an application form and send your film to them on a DVD. There may be a submission fee, so remember to read the rules and regulations of a festival before submitting.

The world's major film festivals are attended by moviemakers and film stars. Here, Brad Pitt is attending the Venice Film Festival. Other major festivals include the Cannes Film Festival and Berlinale in Europe, and the Toronto Film Festival and Sundance in North America.

Film Careers

There are many ways of starting a career in filmmaking. The important thing to decide is what kind of filmmaker you want to be. Do you want to make big, Hollywood-style movies? Do you want to make art films? Or do you want to make documentaries? Find filmmakers who are making the type of movie you want to make and see if you can be an **apprentice**. Volunteer your time, even if it is just for making coffee or running errands. You will learn many valuable skills just by being around the filmmaking process.

Film School

Studying film at college can help you break into the film industry. Some courses are training grounds for major studios, and others encourage students to push the boundaries of film as a form of artistic expression. Some universities focus on screenwriting.

Glossary

apprentice someone who works for a skilled person in order to learn from them.

audition when actors read part of the screenplay in front of the director and producer, who will decide whom to cast.

budget a list of the expenses for each part of a movie.

camera shake the blurring of images that can be caused by using a handheld camera.

celluloid a flexible type of plastic that is used to make movie film.

central crosshatch the box surrounding the central area of an image when seen through a camera's viewfinder.

close-up a type of shot where the camera zooms in close on a subject so that it fills the screen.

color temperature the color of the light. For example, sunlight has a high color temperature, which means that it appears blue.

crew the people who work on a movie, such as the camera operator and director.

develop treating celluloid movie film so that a permanent image appears on it.

diffusion a lighting fixture that scatters the light and prevents glare.

distribute getting a film seen by an audience, whether that is at the movie theater, on television, or through the Internet.

feature films full-length movies, normally of about 80 minutes long or more.

focal length the distance from the surface of a camera's lens to its focal point, which is the film or tape sensor. Focal length determines the angle of view. A wide-angle lens has a short focal length, and a telephoto lens has a long focal length.

f-stop a measurement of the aperture, or opening, of the lens. A low-number f-stop setting gives a wide aperture and lets plenty of light into the lens.

in point when using film-editing software, this marks the start of a clip.

projector a device for showing a movie on a screen.

rigging suspending lights over a film set.

screenplay also called the script, the screenplay is a formatted version of the story, listing who the characters are, what they say, what they do, and where they are doing it.

set the place where a scene is filmed.

showreels video samples of an actor's previous film and television work.

timeline the part of film-editing software where the clips and sequences are put together.

white balance telling the camera what it is to read as pure white in order to adjust for the specific lighting of the set.

Filmmaking Organizations

There are several organizations around the world that offer help and advice to filmmakers of all levels, from small independents to directors wanting to make larger-budget movies.

The Academy of Motion Picture Arts and Sciences (the Oscars) supports and develops film and television work in the United States. It also provides education and opportunities for developing filmmakers.

The Motion Picture Association oversees the distribution and promotion of U.S. films throughout the world.

There are also specialist organizations for each part of the filmmaking process, including the Screenwriters Federation of America and the Directors Guild of America.

Further Reading

Lights, Camera, Action
by Lisa O'Brien (Maple Tree Press, 2007)

Making Short Films: The Complete Guide From Script to Screen
by Clifford Thurlow (Berg Publishers, 2008)

Teach Yourself Film Making
by Tom Holden (McGraw-Hill, 2007)

The Fundamentals of Film Making
by Jane Barnwell (AVA Publishing, 2008)

Web Sites

Due to the changing nature of Internet links, PowerKids Press has developed an online list of Web sites related to the subject of this book. This site is updated regularly. Please use this link to access this list:
http://www.powerkidslinks.com/mt/film

Index